The Book of Matthew

MATTHEW WELTON was born in Nottingham in 1969 and now lives in Manchester. He is an editor of *Stand* magazine and a lecturer in creative writing at Bolton Institute. He has had poems published in the Faber anthology *First Pressings* (1998) and in *New Poetries* II (Carcanet, 1999).

T0167974

MATTHEW WELTON

The Book of Matthew

CARCANET

Acknowledgements

Acknowledgements are made to the editors of *PN Review*, *New Statesman*, *Daily Telegraph*, *New Poetries II* (Carcanet) and *First Pressings* (Faber), and to the organisers of the Eric Gregory Awards, the Arvon Poetry Competition, the National Poetry Competition and the North West Arts Board writers' bursaries.

First published in Great Britain in 2003 by
Carcanet Press Limited
Alliance House
Cross Street
Manchester M2 7AQ

A CIP catalogue record for this book is available from the British Library
ISBN 1 85754 643 1

The publisher acknowledges financial assistance from Arts Council England

Typeset in Monotype Garamond by XL Publishing Services, Tiverton
Printed and bound in England by SRP Ltd, Exeter

Contents

All day I dream about sex

Arrive, and pencil out a list
of things been been, and things been lost.

Then pencil out the pencil-marks
and shade the marks the pencil makes.

So. Wipe the window, latch the lock,
and loop along the mullet-lake.

Or, hang the shirts, unwrap the soap
and scour the skillets. Salt the soup.

Collect the catkins, fresh in bud.
Then tire, and tread at night to bed

in total nightness. Fuse the fuse.
Wake up with the sun on your face.

*

First, buckle on your borrowed shoes
and moon about those morning-shows

with handsome hogs and pissy plots.
And come away, and pick the plates

of mutton-bone, and duckling bones,
and peanut pie, and boiled-down beans.

And dance it from the dining-halls
and hike the humps or lumps of hills.

Then stand, and stand, and hum some hymn.
Then drop like darkness. Heel it home

in summer dimness through the firs.
Wake up with the sun on your face.

Butternuts

The girl who smelled like bubblegum admired the sky.
The telephone rang loudly. Moss grew on the roof.
The neighbours from across the lake would straggle by
for parties in the winter. Pairs of girls would goof

around the gardens where the paths were pebbled green.
The gummy girl would hardly talk. The night it rained
she danced a hula, fingering a tangerine.
She showed her teeth. *The sky is faultless*, she explained.

*

The drunken uncles glooped around the garden-house
then went indoors and offered round their loose cigarettes
and hammered out some practice-piece and sang like cows.
The grey canary-gulls, they said, they kept as pets.

At night a smell like apricots would drowse the rooms.
But now the radio comes on and plays that march
with scrawly cellos, gasps of organ, piles of drums.
The trays of seedlings flourish in the kitchen-porch.

*

All night they talked of breakfast. When the morning came
they cut the meat which tasted more like swedes or beer.
The bony man with monkey teeth was blue as blame,
as caned as custard, juiced as jellied eels. But here

the air takes on the taste of kaolin or yeast
or starch or lemon leaf. The evenings drop like plums.
As spruced as sprouts. As waxed as wasps. Completely spliced.
The breezes soften. Rain comes down. The heating hums.

*

The upstairs smelled of biro-ink. The kitchen smelled
like rained-on wool. The gardens smelled like boiling milk.
The wind that blew blew slowly and the circuits failed.
The rug was rashed with sun. The dark-faced girl would walk

about the bright and rainy streets. She peeled a pear.
The cousins in the kitchen played their reel of tape:
an hour's recorded silence. Shirts hung on a chair.
The sky was deep, and soft. The sky was chocolate soup.

*

The clouds collapse like coals. The sausage-dog that ate
the pears collapses by the trees, then comes inside.
The phone rang loudly. Papers blackened in the grate.
She answered, *Yes. A moment, please* – and walked outside

and swam around the lake. The gardens smelled like tin.
A smudge of sun, a whiff of wind; the rain that falls
falls early in the day. The afternoon wears in.
The shadow shifts in sheets, and daylight blues the walls.

The fundament of wonderment

She said her name was little jones
and bended back her finger-bones

and sang a song in minor thirds.
She spilled a smile and spoke her words.

*

Up here the river turns its boats.
She brings out books of pencil-notes,

her letters from, her letters to,
her clarkesville park, her london zoo.

*

And, in the wind and where she walks
above the blue nasturtium stalks

at london zoo, the smells of apes
are like the smells of table-grapes.

*

The mice and monkeys tell the trees
the wind will end, the worlds will freeze.

She moves herself beyond the grass
the blue boats pass. The blue boats pass.

Van der Kerkhoff

It matters how some afternoon late into spring
the voices round the cafe tables lift and fall
like sea birds or low winds, and a smudge of orange light

plays slowly through the window; and it matters how
the houses along the yellow ocean, drifting out
of darkness as the day assembles over the hills,

seem, kind of, to draw quietly backward from the beach;
and, also, in the months between the summers, with
the weather in the zeros and the starch-colour cloud

absorbing into the evening sky, it matters how
the conversation in the kitchen falls towards
the need to know – *in the unendingness of God*

where is it man begins? – and what else matters is
the crazed, credential sun; the insects around the trees;
the chance of rain; the shadows in the short, chalky grass.

Well get this then – I love you, were the Woody's words.
Tobacco bushes flowered in the pebbly soil.
The day came like electric heat. Swallows flew low.
The soup shop at the corner smelled like noodle soup
or spinach with asparagus and eggs and cream.
The Woody lit a small cigarette, and breathed out hard.

This woman there with squiggles in her hair makes moves
that get the Woody in a squirm: *the smiles she curves
across her mouth*, he means, and how sometimes the sun
burns hazy all the morning and by afternoon
the flowers open slowly in the window where
melodically and thoughtfully she hums out loud.

*Vodka, she likes. Whisky also. And plums. And limes.
And lemon-peel. Fried fruit. Dry beans. Deep soup. Warm cream.*
The Woody gets to talking in that buzzy voice
he uses when he's fucking, though it's been some time,
and as the wind wears off like drunkenness or lust
his thoughts burn out like lightbulbs and the daytime fades.

The soup the Woody simmers in the soup shop in
the evening has a taste like turps or tartrazine
that keeps him from his sleep. *What bloody soup is that?
What light through eggs asparagus? How came spinach?*
The day comes like some kind of marijuana high
and almost nearly keeps him kind of sort of blue.

The Woody don't get well no more, and while the sun
sits simply in the space above the cuckoo-trees
and gooey soup-smells drift along the shallow winds
and fishes float in figure-eights and hawklings hear
how sparrows speak and somewhere in the narrow hills
summer begins, the Woody just can't keep from cryin'.

The clouds come out like flowers and the days don't last.
The bushes fill with wind. *My words*, the Woody said,
come slower in the summer. And the sounds his words
make kind of get the woman sort of almost high,
as tunefully she hums him something sweet and sad,
just here, and now he's gone, and now he's nowhere.

Dozen

the thoughts flustering like the wind around these gardens
overlooking the sea
the thoughts these children described with a fingers-in-a-hornet-hole
kind of a hubbub

the thoughts we went through that first summer of the
grasshopper-fever epidemic
the thoughts the girl in the tennis-dress was anxious to make
understood

those thoughts coming out in tangles as we sat together in silence
the thoughts we got onto as we hurried out to the roof

the thoughts taking shape as we queued silently for pastries this
morning
the thoughts communicated by an abrupt or showy quickening of
the breath

the thoughts we went into over that supper of artichokes and
spaghetti
the thoughts expanded upon in *chaoticism and opportunity in the indian raj*

the thoughts copied out into the fly-leaves of the *contemporary colorists*
year-book
the thoughts wafting through the mind like this lemons-and-
burned-sugar kind of smell

the thoughts muddling around the mind like the shadows inside our
room
the thought of a fat man speaking quietly with a thin man

the thoughts set out in later editions of *the daubist movement manifesto*
the thoughts which make their visit during these closing moments
of sleep

the thoughts spoken into a telephone outside a room somewhere in
iraq
the thoughts we discuss over lunch, a little drunken on
hickory-flavour beer

these thoughts taking shape as a slow yellow sunlight thickens the
                                                          windows
that thought which yesterday came to us as we were driving west

the thought involved in remembering why it was we ever left honolulu
the thoughts dismantled like bicycle-parts one idle spring morning
                                                    around tel aviv

the thoughts borrowed from the books we found sunning in the
                                                          window
the thoughts we recollect from our afternoons of frantic and
                                                    loving sex

these thoughts like clouds that lie like dead dogs in the sky
these thoughts which translate into a feverish low-pitched melodic
                                                    kind of buzz

Tighten up

The sound the aeroplane above the city makes
moves gorgeously around these slim apartment blocks.

The taste of lithic metals, cobalts, ferrics, zincs
approximates the sweetness of these herring chunks.

The alder bushes lose their good hard-onions smell;
the shadow of a wood-hawk lifts against the wall.

A slack, oxidic water and a firm warm wind
swell gradually all morning at this slow-banked pond.

The cellist dims the pigeon-lamps.
Demurely, in the garden-camps

the shapes of trees the light allows
unfold the fruits the bluefowls browse.

The melody the morning hums
comes only as an old thought comes.

*

The oboist who blows his cloud
of oboe-notes and leaves them loud

observes the way the garden-rooks
fall from the air. The kitchen-books

observe how well a candle's heat
will fricassee fresh sparrow-meat.

*

Comes only as an old thought comes.
The symphonist demurely drums

these meanings which the morning sings.
These meanings which the morning brings

bring with them clouds of flies and bees
and bluish light and bluish trees.

*

Comes only as the sounds from words,
as flutterings of floating birds

above the camps of clumsy cows.
Comes only as this light allows,

as clumsy strums by thicker thumbs
in thickish light. But comes. But comes.

Van der Kerkhoff

It matters how some afternoon late into spring
the voices round the cafe tables lift and fall
like sea birds or low winds, and a smudge of orange light

plays slowly through the window; and it matters how
the houses along the yellow ocean, drifting out
of darkness as the day assembles over the hills,

seem, kind of, to draw quietly backward from the beach;
and, also, in the months between the summers, with
the weather in the zeros and the starch-colour cloud

absorbing into the evening sky, it matters how
the conversation in the kitchen falls towards
the need to know – *in the unendingness of God*

where is it man begins? – and what else matters is
the crazed credential, sun; the insects around the trees;
the chance of rain; the shadows in the short, chalky grass.

London sundays

Snatches of summer in afternoon parks
are probably now as good as it gets.
Meeting beneath the clock that never works
then sloping off homewards as the sun sets
behind the bandstand must be the closest
anyone can come to finding again
that good, good feeling that will last and last
like a child's holidays. Dusk comes. Then rain.

And love never really feels like some craze
that hits like gin, buzzes like benzedrine,
and smells as good as coffee. In some ways
all it has to be is something between
a half-funny joke and some old rumour
from somewhere around, that arrives unrushed
like boredom, wears on like a bad winter,
and which spreads through rooms like sunlight and dust.

Springtime

She only lives a street or two away.
Still, every day there's something in the mail –

a picture-card without too much to say,
just where she's been and who she's seen, that's all.

She never telephones or comes around.
This morning where the postman left his bike

the shadow that it spread along the ground
was hardly there, and no one was awake.

President Marbles

Or the wednesday morning, or the orange-lime rinds,
or the frog-fish, or the fiver folded lengthways,
or the puffball mushrooms, or the silent house-guests,
or the fractured lightbulb, or the cornflakes with cream.

Or the sturdy, sturdy girl with the folded hands,
or the chicory-cheese, or the short avenues,
or the puddle-mud, or the children with fat wrists,
or the pint of tea, or the large pineapple farm.

Or, in the dusk-brown dip of evening, skanking off
by the perch-ponds, or holing up at the fives-hall.
The shirt-paper. The gimbal-stove. The duff-pastry.
The juniper-juice. Or, alone here in the road,

the goony girl, the gusty girl, the huffy guff.
The gumptious girl. That total gaggle of a girl.
The gummy girl. The gloomy girl. The hickory.
The limb-loose girl with teeth like nuts. That pebblehead.

Or the dead dozen daisy-pans. The wrap of zap.
The little muff of roll-your-own. Or those crew-necks.
Or the chicken-shit father, the chicken-shit son.
The tree on the square. This woman who wouldn't kiss.

The you-are-here map. The penny-slot telescope.
The sheet-music. The chocolate-box instamatics.
These breakfast-plates. That photograph signed with crayon.
The room with the willow-wood chair. This lightlessness.

'What utters winters'

What utters winters, brings springs, lays the summer's days
and shortens resolutely autumn's afternoons;

what places in this air these birds, or in these birds
the will to wander in this air; what gives light light,

makes wind come, causes leaves to fall, or trees to rise
or lakes to swell or to the sun affords this sense

of issuing these fields and ponds and sands and woods
makes, where it makes a thing, the thing part-incomplete,

allowing for how anything must on its own
include some need, the way the thing which shapes the heart

figures it less than whole, or figures it so made
that constantly it wants this hard, redemptive hurt

which only some glimpsed, ingredient heart can provide
and which, perhaps, birds find issuing from the sun.

Sometimes I see me dead in the rain

Ecclesiastes Malin at the hills behind the house.
Ecclesiastes Malin in the river. Treading mud.
Talking through his teeth. At day, laying out the whittleknife.
Returning from the lower rooms with sugar on his breath.

Ecclesiastes Malin with that look that leaves his face
resembling something scorched, or something strained, or
                                        something soured.
And as it comes to darkness, whispering quickly to himself.
Ecclesiastes Malin with his fist inside his mouth.

                    *

The way the morning brings the wind that smells like berryfruit.
Those goatbones in the yard. The little scale of blackbirdsong.
A greenness to this light. A slowness to the evening wind
that stirs the clouds. The sun across his face, at night the moon.

These dawns and noons, these dusks that come. The simple falls
                                        of night.
The millpool and its minnowfish. The dusts the noontimes bring.
These apples hung above the stream. The hackknife in his hand.
The wind all night. Ecclesiastes nowhere to be seen.

                    *

Ecclesiastes Malin with his fingers in this tree
whose branches lend their shadows down the paths across the fields,
that buds and leafs, growing a fruit that looks like fruit gone bad.
This sense of evening settled in the woods along the hill.

And smoke that rises. Rain that falls. The wind that dries the air.
These things that bring Ecclesiastes silent to these roads,
across this sunned-in square, beneath the turning weatherbird.
These things that see Ecclesiastes whistling at the wall.

                    *

The woods acquiring darkness as his bones take on the cold,
The way the morning takes its dampness from the dwindled night.
The summer has him moving slowly, spitting like a hen.
The summer has him waking in the drying heathergrass.

The winds that breeze above the stream. The stream that cuts
                                                  the fields.
Tickling grayling. Eyeing the sun. Untethering a boat.
Ecclesiastes chewing chalk. A greyness to the rain.
And furrowed cloud. And birdcall in the night. And littler stars.

De Boer

It matters how some afternoon late into spring
the voices round the cafe tables lift and fall
like sea birds or low winds, and a smudge of orange light

plays slowly through the window; and it matters how
the houses along the yellow ocean, drifting out
of darkness as the day assembles over the hills,

seem, kind of, to draw quietly backward from the beach;
and, also, in the months between the summers, with
the weather in the zeros and the starch-colour cloud

absorbing into the evening sky, it matters how
the conversation in the kitchen falls towards
the need to know – *in the unendingness of God*

where is it man begins? – and what else matters is
the still, uncertain air; the insects around the trees;
the chance of rain; the shadows in the short, chalky grass.

Colors

i   Buttery chocolate, whisky and muscovado, and
peaches and honey, and caramel.

ii   Orange-skins and chocolate, and gravelly whisky,
coffee-flavour, nectarines and honey.

Hubba

The woods above the river in these apple-winds
make autumn feel too much like spring. If this was where
we wintered in that tall hotel the wood surrounds
we wouldn't know it now. A smell like salted beer
came warmly from the corridor. We stayed a week
then tipped the clerk to move us to the floor above.
As evening breaks we'll drive the slow way from the lake.
The last time we were here we almost didn't leave.

Octobering away from town in borrowed rooms,
by day we barely speak; at night we talk and talk
until again we're silent and the daylight comes.
We make our old mistake of ever going back
and find addresses wiped to demolition sites,
the same grey headache washing through the afternoons.
We stay among the architects in city flats.
We wander in the woodland where the slow stream runs.

But probably the journeys that we mean to make
and somehow never do would bring us here the same.
Those evenings in that house the smell of peachwood-smoke
amounted to a feeling like some sense of calm,
as if some slow or natural wind, some cleaner light,
had brought us to some answer, to some sure because,
and though the lease was paid, the season wasn't out
and we were tooling down the coast-road, pleased as geese.

The looseness of our clothes; the faded fabric sky;
the thin-aired winter – mashed potatoes, hurried sex;
the way the sea reflects the sky, the sky the sea;
and milk-blue morning mist; and yards with cars on bricks;
and houses burned away; and wind against our teeth;
the doctor's friends whose conversation drifts like sand;
the wordless girl who breathed the way that goldfish breathe;
the clouds rummaging the sky: these things come to mind.

And here at last, alone, we fill our coffee cups
and, standing at the window in the kitchen-lounge,
we find it easier to see how one thing slips
into another, simpler to believe in change,
and difficult to know for sure if what we feel
is autumn coming on or summer at its close.
At night we notice tiny birds circling the hill,
the echo from the road, the wind among the stars.

Another explanation

The lemon-colour river in the hour after dawn
following down around the low-hilled city as these
warm papery breezes soften into the air

seems to have about it something almost like
a kind of illogic – the denial, perhaps, of
any sense of order, any order of sense –

so that where it swells or slackens or
gives back this glare or where it reflects
the boats it gives this shrugging motion, it

seems almost to be holding something back.
The daylight saddens. The breezes shift. Above
the avenues a mumbling sound carries across the air.

Where the poplar-trees line up around the gravel park
the swallows lull into the wind and
the gluey still-cola smell drifting from

the lifted windows of the main street coffee-lofts
comes almost like something final, sifting onto
the breeze as the air begins to cloud and

the river widens and slows, its new deep-yellow colour
glimmering a little in the swells and flows of light.

Parlour trick

The mirror in the hall reflects the spread
of junk and clutter through the room: the bed
pushed up against the wall, the paper plants,
the drop-leaf table, photos, ornaments.
A square of sunlight lengthens on the floor.

The radio, left on, purrs out some slow
six-eight, the cello with that wheezy, low
morendo that's so popular these days.
Roll up the rug, push back the chairs, this place
might make some party: dancing, drinks, the door

open onto the lawn, some darling draped
along the couch, the wall-lights dimmed. Except
if anybody did come in they'd find
the pages of the calendar unturned,
the apples clenched up in the bowl, the bulbs

all blown. The sunlight in the curtain blurs.
The lily-water yellows in the vase.
A smell like soil hangs loosely in the air.
The shelves are piled with papers; on the chair,
an uncleared plate, an ashtray filled with stubs.

The concert

I don't know what she said. A bleachy light
was spreading from the house across the lawn.
The trees were full of birds. It wasn't late.

We listened to the concert, then the news.
Then, in the thirty minutes that the sun
was squinting in the windows and the noise

the traffic made was lifting to these cold
uncurtained rooms, she sat down with the phone.
She talked and talked and talked. I'm not sure who she called.

Driving slow

Linus and Lucy
Linus and Lucy
Linus and Lucy
Linus and Lucy
Linus and Lucy
Linus and Lucy

Linus and Lucy
Linus and Lucy
Linus and Lucy
Linus and Lucy
Linus and Lucy
Linus and Lucy

Linus and Lucy
Linus and Lucy
Linus and Lucy
Linus and Lucy
Linus and Lucy
Linus and Lucy

Linus and Lucy
Linus and Lucy
Linus and Lucy
Linus and Lucy
Linus and Lucy
Linus and Lucy

Linus and Lucy
Linus and Lucy
Linus and Lucy
Linus and Lucy
Linus and Lucy
Linus and Lucy

Linus and Lucy
Linus and Lucy
Linus and Lucy
Linus and Lucy
Linus and Lucy
Linus and Lucy

De Boer

It matters how some afternoon late into spring
the voices round the cafe tables lift and fall
like sea birds or low winds, and a smudge of orange light

plays slowly through the window; and it matters how
the houses along the yellow ocean, drifting out
of darkness as the day assembles over the hills,

seem, kind of, to draw quietly backward from the beach;
and, also, in the months between the summers, with
the weather in the zeros and the starch-colour cloud

absorbing into the evening sky, it matters how
the conversation in the kitchen falls towards
the need to know – *in the unendingness of God*

where is it man begins? – and what else matters is
the still-uncertain air; the insects around the trees;
the chance of rain; the shadows in the short, chalky grass.

Two hands

noon

The dizzy girl walked quickly down the beach.

1.05

The roads were slow. The fields were full of fruit.
The smiling boy drove up beside the beach.

2.11

The landlord turned the lightswitch on the wall.
The room was dark and smelled of winter fruit.
They pulled the shade and watched the empty beach.

3.16

She spoke his name and walked across the room
and did him quickly up against the wall.
They lit cigarettes and shared a piece of fruit.
He talked. She stared outside, towards the beach.

4.22

The bulky policeman made his usual rounds –
the dairy yard, the parks, the snooker rooms.
He turned and moved towards the warehouse walls,
the market stands, the yellow fish, the fruit,
and took the quick way back, along the beach.

5.27

He talked about a place they used to know
– his smile grew dim, her eyes became less round –
his cousin's house a mile from here, the rooms
he'd decorate each spring, the garden walls,
the pond with frogs, the yard that stank like fruit,
the fires they'd make with driftwood from the beach.

6.33

She told him as she leaned against the stairs
it's not the only house she's ever known.
She talked about a street where friends came round,
an orchestra, a city where her room
was clean and cheap, with nothing on the walls.
And coming home, her face as bruised as fruit.
And pacing down the beach, the bastard beach.

7.38

For him these furnished evenings never match
that kick, that itch, of shuffling up the stairs
and listening for some voice you think you know,
of knocking once, then twice, then slipping round
the back, of chasing through the basement rooms,
of forcing doors, of slamming into walls,
of striking matches, crouched in crates of fruit,
of watching from the warehouse by the beach.

8.43

The room grew darker. Cars went by outside.
For everything that's wrong he struck a match:
that ugly mary coming up the stairs,
the radio with songs you think you know,
the tenants' goosey daughters hanging round,
the syrup-marmalade, the breakfast room,
the landlord with a glass against the wall,
the typing-paper bedsheets, polished fruit,
the photographs of donkeys on the beach.

9.49

A panda car drew up across the street.
The bars were full, with people stood outside.
The moon was slim, and dimmer than a match,
and while the smiling boy cut down the stairs
and dogged about as if he doesn't know
the way from here, the ambulance pulled round
the front and stopped outside the function room.
He carried on and waited by the wall,
then kicked his way among the rinds of fruit
that washed along the edges of the beach.

10.54

She caught her own reflection in the glass
and stopped a moment, staring at the street.
She sat and smoked. A light came on outside.
She moved her mouth. She lit a kitchen match.
She swore out loud. She whispered down the stairs
and rattled off about some girl she knew.
She spent a moment sparrowing around
with keys and coins and cases through the room.
She hung a pocket mirror on the wall
and hacked her hair and finished up the fruit.
She left, and pounded down the muddy beach.

midnight

She hurried past the promenade, the pier,
and joined him in the cafe for a glass
of milk. He took her arm, and crossed the street
and put her in a cab. He slipped inside
the boarding house. He tried to get a match
to light. He slumped off down the cellar stairs.

The roads were blocked. The driver said he knew
an easier way and turned the taxi round.

The landlord found the policeman in the room
behind the snooker club. He thumped the wall
until his hands were raw and ripe, like fruit.
He took the slow way back, along the beach.

The wonderment of fundament

Early in spring the weather hasn't changed.
The concert-room is peppishness unhinged.

Tonight the lady pianist who plays
con fuoco hardly hears her own applause.

*

A Mr Macaroni stops his Ford
two streets away and lets the engine flood,

the radio just loud enough to hear,
one crate of pippin-apples, one of beer.

*

She makes her music, loosening her hands.
The moment holds. But if the evening ends,

the coffee-place will crowd, and trains will leave,
and fields absorb what light the moon might give.

*

These city birds among these city trees
sing slow above this greyness in the grass,

and Mr Macaroni pours his beer
and rattles apples up against his ear.

An ABC of American suicide

Arbus

The skies are stuffed with bread-coloured clouds and huge, huge
                                          raindrops
spill like peach-juice. Anyone who was hurrying to meet
a friend by the Central Park Zoo birdhouse might have to stop,
check themselves, and walk right on before they found they'd
                                          just spent
one whole hour watching fat cigar-smoke skimming from the neat
nutmeggy mouth of that mud-eyed girl that those two boy-scouts
can't get enough of. Even when they arrive home they can't
stop talking about her. They fidget like jumping-beans, pout
like movie-stars, but sleep like piglets 'til their parents slam
in, late from some gallery-crowd party in a back-stairs
apartment on Fifty-seventh. Through suitcase-cardboard walls
their half-high father grinds on about cocktails and cab-fares,
groaning like a gramophone with a faulty repeat-arm.

Brautigan

San Francisco: the morning arriving on Beaver Street
like just-percolating coffee; the early-day sunshine
hanging around like a catchy tune; the afternoon heat
building and building and growing huge like an easy yawn.
In the Ceiling-Fan Luncheonette, quart jars of Mad Dog wine
and half-packs of pocket-crushed Winstons pass from college kid
to college kid and everyone spoons into hot popcorn.
Skinny boys stretch out fudgy stories about what they did
all summer, bumming truck rides south and getting themselves lost.
Evening comes on like a sudden tiredness; the sky becomes
a smear of cinnamon-paste. Girls head home to make phone-calls
and down by the bay the streets are empty but for the bums
and dogs and wind and litter and dust, american dust.

Cobain

The wow-eyed boy in the horse-chestnut shoes tears a grapefruit
to pieces, throws a corn-cob smile to a nearby stranger,
pulls his pennies-and-dimes bicycle from the ground, and scoots
southwards from the square 'til the monument he's spent the day
swinging his legs from is half-an-hour behind him. Later,
sat on the whitewashed window-sill of someone else's room,
clutching the phone, he gives a howl that could scare snakes away
and hangs up. He says something about finding his way home
then laughs himself to the floor. He looks up with a quick smirk
and makes for town to see someone who meets him with a kiss.
By a park that's sprinkled with a doughnut-sugar snowfall
he turns to his friend and wonders out loud, *With days like this
as cheap as chewing-gum, why would anyone want to work?*

The bees all morning contemplate how slow things are
and hover off above the hills, in Rafi's thoughts.
Those bees, thinks Rafi slowly, move their minds like mud.

*

Rafi all morning moves his things around the floor,
the thought-up things he sits alone and contemplates.
A bee comes by. The hills emerge through drifts of cloud.

*

What Hannah has Liat has, and what Hannah has
some mornings in the hills in terracotta bowls
is apple-coloured melon-halves she eats with glee.

*

The holes below the hills are full of sleeping bees
and Rafi hovers off alone as sunlight falls,
Liat says, Hannah says. A cloud comes slowly by.

*

The bees suppose a fondness for the sunlit hills
the sunlit melons roll around. The sunlight curves
like bubbling mud, Liat supposes Hannah says.

*

Liat emerges from the terracotta holes
and contemplates the apple-coloured melon-halves.
The sunlight curves, the bees suppose, the bees suppose.

The book of Matthew

Class one: Abstract relations

Section 1: Existence

The wind around the orange-tree
brings on the smell
of nutskins mixed with whisky

mixed with lemons or rain,
and carries through
the grasses where the flowers

in the sun redden a little
and the shadows unfold.
The slow, late-morning light

collecting above the brackens and
brambles comes strongest
where the tangle-plants

bundle out over the lawns,
glimmering like sugar
in the fuller, warmer air.

Quietly thunder-bugs
mumble in the heat; butter-paper
clouds gather low in the sky.

And it is the wind – narrowing in
like something in the mind,
and carrying with it this applewood

kind of smell – that makes the mood
that makes the day
feel actual or eternal

or formal or real. Below the trees
the shadow puddles out.
Unhurriedly the light passes. Unhurriedly

the wind loosens off into the day.
The sound of insects
carries hesitantly into the air.

Section 2: Relation

The wind around the orange-tree
brings on a smell
like caramel or kedgeree

or rubber or gum,
and carries through
the orchards where the flowers

in the sun gladden a little
and the shadows unroll.
The slow, late-morning light

collecting above the brackens and
brambles comes firmest
where the spindle-plants

bundle out over the lawns,
glimmering like sugar
in the fuller, drier air.

Quietly slumber-bugs
mumble in the heat; crayon-paper
clouds gather low in the sky.

And it is the wind – levelling out
like something in the mind,
and carrying with it this larchwood

kind of smell – that makes the mood
that makes the day
feel solid and constant,

original and plain. Below the trees
the shadow puddles out.
Hesitantly the light passes. Hesitantly

the wind loosens off into the day.
The sound of insects
carries deliberately into the air.

Section 3: Quantity

The wind around the orange-tree
brings on a smell
like savlon or aspirin

or brick-damp or enamel,
and carries through
the nettles where the flowers

in the sun stiffen a little
and the shadows unwind.
The slow, late-morning light

collecting above the brackens and
brambles comes surest
where the turtle-plants

bundle out over the lawns,
glimmering like sugar
in the fuller, clearer air.

Quietly hover-bugs
mumble in the heat; cotton-paper
clouds gather low in the sky.

And it is the wind – lowering in
like something in the mind,
and carrying with it this rubber-wood

kind of smell – that makes the mood
that makes the day
feel simple and infinite,

certain and absolute. Below the trees
the shadow puddles out.
Deliberately the light passes. Deliberately

the wind loosens off into the day.
The sound of insects
carries stubbornly into the air.

The wind around the orange-tree
brings on a smell
like coffee or yogurt

or lemonade or rusks,
and carries through
the bean-vines where the flowers

in the sun shudder a little
and the shadows unspool.
The slow, late-morning light

collecting above the brackens and
brambles comes bluest
where the pencil-plants

bundle out over the lawns,
glimmering like sugar
in the fuller, wider air.

Quietly tinder-bugs
mumble in the heat; grocer-paper
clouds gather low in the sky.

And it is the wind – opening out
like something in the mind,
and carrying with it this fruitwood

kind of smell – that makes the mood
that makes the day
feel harmonious and symmetrical,

concordant and precise. Below the trees
the shadow puddles out.
Stubbornly the light passes. Stubbornly

the wind loosens off into the day.
The sound of insects
carries unfussily into the air.

The wind around the orange-tree
brings on a smell
like warm cream or soft sugar

or nougat or fudge,
and carries through
the rushes where the flowers

in the sun weary a little
and the shadows expand.
The slow, late-morning light

collecting above the brackens and
brambles comes plainest
where the panda-plants

bundle out over the lawns,
glimmering like sugar
in the fuller, bluer air.

Quietly rhumba-bugs
mumble in the heat; dust-paper
clouds gather low in the sky.

And it is the wind – rumbling away
like something in the mind,
and carrying with it this nut-wood

kind of smell – that makes the mood
that makes the day
feel unitary and even,

arithmetical and whole. Below the trees
the shadow puddles out.
Unfussily the light passes. Unfussily

the wind loosens off into the day.
The sound of insects
carries softly into the air.

Section 6: Time

The wind around the orange-tree
brings on a smell
like lanolin or hessian

or toothpaste or chalk,
and carries through
the willows where the flowers

in the sun colour a little
and the shadows extend.
The slow, late-morning light

collecting above the brackens and
brambles comes wholest
where the paddle-plants

bundle out over the lawns,
glimmering like sugar
in the fuller, realer air.

Quietly mambo-bugs
mumble in the heat; bleach-paper
clouds gather low in the sky.

And it is the wind – rambling around
like something in the mind,
and carrying with it this pinewood

kind of smell – that makes the mood
that makes the day
feel present and permanent,

perpetual and prime. Below the trees
the shadow puddles out.
Softly the light passes. Softly

the wind loosens off into the day.
The sound of insects
carries comfortably into the air.

Section 7: Change

The wind around the orange-tree
brings on a smell
like vermouth or molasses

or nutmeg or rum,
and carries through
the hedges where the flowers

in the sun dwindle a little
and the shadows fade.
The slow, late-morning light

collecting above the brackens and
brambles comes oftenest
where the parcel-plants

bundle out over the lawns,
glimmering like sugar
in the fuller, wholer air.

Quietly lumber-bugs
mumble in the heat; wax-paper
clouds gather low in the sky.

And it is the wind – hustling in
like something in the mind,
and carrying with it this birchwood

kind of smell – that makes the mood
that makes the day
feel inviolate and necessary,

fixed and complete. Below the trees
the shadow puddles out.
Comfortably the light passes. Comfortably

the wind loosens off into the day.
The sound of insects
carries weakly into the air.

Section 8: Causation

The wind around the orange-tree
brings on a smell
like talcum or putty

or diesel or schmaltz,
and carries through
the mosses where the flowers

in the sun straggle a little
and the shadows return.
The slow, late-morning light

collecting above the brackens and
brambles comes realest
where the rattle-plants

bundle out over the lawns,
glimmering like sugar
in the fuller, nearer air.

Quietly button-bugs
mumble in the heat; baking-paper
clouds gather low in the sky.

And it is the wind – holding off
like something in the mind,
and carrying with it this rowan-wood

kind of smell – that makes the mood
that makes the day
feel intrinsic and dynamic,

fundamental and primordial. Below the trees
the shadow puddles out.
Weakly the light passes. Weakly

the wind loosens off into the day.
The sound of insects
carries imprecisely into the air.

Class two: Space

Section 1: Space in general

The skies above the orange-tree
bring in a smell
like goat-dirt or cow-dirt

or bird-dirt or horse-dirt
which carries through
the orchards where the grasses

in the sun tangle a little
and the shadows collect.
The clear, late-morning light

resettling above the brackens and
brambles glows reddest
where the poodle-plants

bundle out over the lawns,
shining like sugar
in the warmer, drier air.

Frantically number-bugs
tumble in the heat; flower-paper
clouds gather low in the sky.

And it is the wind – coming on
like something in the mind,
and carrying with it this palm-wood

kind of smell – that makes the mood
that makes the day
feel obvious and ubiquitous,

architectural and universal. Below the trees
the shadow puddles out.
Imprecisely the light passes. Imprecisely

the wind loosens off into the day.
The sound of insects
carries delicately into the air.

Section 2: Dimensions

The skies above the orange-tree
bring in a smell
like polythene or plasticine

or barbiturates or band-aids
which carries through
the nettles where the grasses

in the sun thicken a little
and the shadows relax.
The clear, late-morning light

resettling above the brackens and
brambles glows briefest
where the whittle-plants

bundle out over the lawns,
shining like sugar
in the warmer, clearer air.

Frantically bumble-bugs
tumble in the heat; reefer-paper
clouds gather low in the sky.

And it is the wind – fastening in
like something in the mind,
and carrying with it this gum-wood

kind of smell – that makes the mood
that makes the day
feel weighty and lengthy

and distant and removed. Below the trees
the shadow puddles out.
Delicately the light passes. Delicately

the wind loosens off into the day.
The sound of insects
carries uncertainly into the air.

The skies above the orange-tree
bring in a smell
like butter or buckwheat

or barley or bran
that carries through
the bean-vines where the grasses

in the sun flatten a little
and the shadows emerge.
The clear, late-morning light

resettling above the brackens and
brambles glows longest
where the lobster-plants

bundle out over the lawns,
shining like sugar
in the warmer, wider air.

Frantically pillow-bugs
tumble in the heat; russia-paper
clouds gather low in the sky.

And it is the wind – brushing by
like something in the mind,
and carrying with it this softwood

kind of smell – that makes the mood
that makes the day
feel rigid and regular,

structural and straight. Below the trees
the shadow puddles out.
Uncertainly the light passes. Uncertainly

the wind loosens off into the day.
The sound of insects
carries vaguely into the air.

Section 4: Motion

The skies above the orange-tree
bring in the smell
of lunch-rooms and soup-rooms

and games-rooms and book-rooms
that carries through
the rushes where the grasses

in the sun fluster a little
and the shadows recede.
The clear, late-morning light

resettling above the brackens and
brambles glows fullest
where the needle-plants

bundle out over the lawns,
shining like sugar
in the warmer, bluer air.

Frantically rhino-bugs
tumble in the heat; pickle-paper
clouds gather low in the sky.

And it is the wind – rushing through
like something in the mind,
and carrying with it this jack-wood

kind of smell – that makes the mood
that makes the day
feel elastic and erratic,

diverted and unquiet. Below the trees
the shadow puddles out.
Vaguely the light passes. Vaguely

the wind loosens off into the day.
The sound of insects
carries reluctantly into the air.

Class three: Matter

Section 1: Matter in general

The breeze about the orange-tree
brings up a smell
like sticking plasters or washed cotton,

lit matches or antiseptic,
and carries through
the nettles where the orchards

in the sun rustle a little
and the shadows revolve.
The soft, late-morning light

refracting above the brackens and
brambles falls furthest
where the poker-plants

bundle out over the lawns,
softening like sugar
in the drier, clearer air.

Hazily meadow-bugs
fumble in the heat; apple-paper
clouds gather low in the sky.

And it is the wind – filling out
like something in the mind,
and carrying with it this hardwood

kind of smell – that makes the mood
that makes the day
feel tangible and physical,

material and concrete. Below the trees
the shadow puddles out.
Reluctantly the light passes. Reluctantly

the wind loosens off into the day.
The sound of insects
carries eventually into the air.

Section 2: Inorganic matter

The breeze about the orange-tree
brings up a smell
like apple-sap or calvados

or melons or figs,
and carries through
the bean-vines where the orchards

in the sun densen a little
and the shadows distort.
The soft, late-morning light

refracting above the brackens and
brambles falls latest
where the tiger-plants

bundle out over the lawns,
softening like sugar
in the drier, wider air.

Hazily berry-bugs
fumble in the heat; lemon-paper
clouds gather low in the sky.

And it is the wind – loafing about
like something in the mind,
and carrying with it this burned-wood

kind of smell – that makes the mood
that makes the day
feel curdy and soupy

and lumpy and muggy. Below the trees
the shadow puddles out.
Eventually the light passes. Eventually

the wind loosens off into the day.
The sound of insects
carries fussily into the air.

Section 3: Organic matter

The breeze about the orange-tree
brings up a smell
like proteins and paraffin,

glycerine or turpentine,
and carries through
the rushes where the orchards

in the sun huddle a little
and the shadows return.
The soft, late-morning light

refracting above the brackens and
brambles falls nearest
where the sparrow-plants

bundle out over the lawns,
softening like sugar
in the drier, bluer air.

Hazily picnic-bugs
fumble in the heat; orange-paper
clouds gather low in the sky.

And it is the wind – happening by
like something in the mind,
and carrying with it this ash-wood

kind of smell – that makes the mood
that makes the day
feel muffled and mellow

and lucid and light. Below the trees
the shadow puddles out.
Fussily the light passes. Fussily

the wind loosens off into the day.
The sound of insects
carries hazily into the air.

Class four: Intellect: The exercise of the mind

Division one: Formation of ideas

Section 1: General

The girl beneath the orange-tree
makes out the smell
of crayon-wax mixed with canvas

mixed with linseed or ink
that follows through
the bean-vines where the nettles

in the sun tremble a little
and the shadows revive.
The clean, late-morning light

reflected above the brackens and
brambles feels brightest
where the yaffle-plants

bundle out over the lawns,
jellying like sugar
in the clearer, wider air.

Raucously truffle-bugs
rumble in the heat; studio-paper
clouds gather low in the sky.

And it is the wind – following on
like something in the mind,
and carrying with it this magnolia

kind of smell – that makes the mood
that makes the day
feel conceptual and rational,

logical and philosophic. Below the trees
the shadow puddles out.
Hazily the light passes. Hazily

the wind slackens off into the morning.
The sound of insects
carries unclearly into the air.

The girl beneath the orange-tree
makes out the smell
of dextrose or glucose

or lactose or sucrose
that follows through
the rushes where the nettles

in the sun swagger a little
and the shadows contract.
The clean, late-morning light

reflected above the brackens and
brambles feels closest
where the candle-plants

bundle out over the lawns,
jellying like sugar
in the clearer, bluer air.

Raucously idiot-bugs
rumble in the heat; butcher-paper
clouds gather low in the sky.

And it is the wind – colouring out
like something in the mind,
and carrying with it this maple-nut

kind of smell – that makes the mood
that makes the day
feel meticulous and particular,

pedantic and minute. Below the trees
the shadow puddles out.
Unclearly the light passes. Unclearly

the wind slackens off into the morning.
The sound of insects
carries quietly into the air.

Section 3: Materials for reasoning

The girl beneath the orange-tree
makes out the smell
old furniture gives off

on rainy summer days
which follows through
the willows where the nettles

in the sun brighten a little
and the shadows collapse.
The clean, late-morning light

reflected above the brackens and
brambles feels truest
where the hammer-plants

bundle out over the lawns,
jellying like sugar
in the clearer, realer air.

Raucously beer-bugs
rumble in the heat; zinc-paper
clouds gather low in the sky.

And it is the wind – carrying out
like something in the mind,
and carrying with it this beechy

kind of smell – that makes the mood
that makes the day
feel suggestive or significant,

meaningful or final. Below the trees
the shadow puddles out.
Quietly the light passes. Quietly

the wind slackens off into the morning.
The sound of insects
carries cautiously into the air.

The girl beneath the orange-tree
makes out the smell
of fish-skins or egg-skins

or fruit-skins or bean-skins
that follows through
the hedges where the nettles

in the sun harden a little
and the shadows relent.
The clean, late-morning light

reflected above the brackens and
brambles feels bleakest
where the penguin-plants

bundle out over the lawns,
jellying like sugar
in the clearer, wholer air.

Raucously bundle-bugs
rumble in the heat; letter-paper
clouds gather low in the sky.

And it is the wind – faltering on
like something in the mind,
and carrying with it this sallowy

kind of smell – that makes the mood
that makes the day
feel dialectic or deductive,

inferential or analytic. Below the trees
the shadow puddles out.
Cautiously the light passes. Cautiously

the wind slackens off into the morning.
The sound of insects
carries numbly into the air.

Section 5: Results of reasoning

The girl beneath the orange-tree
makes out the smell
of pianos or satchels

or vinegar or rust
that follows through
the mosses where the nettles

in the sun waggle a little
and the shadows unfurl.
The clean, late-morning light

reflected above the brackens and
brambles feels newest
where the dandle-plants

bundle out over the lawns,
jellying like sugar
in the clearer, nearer air.

Raucously cola-bugs
rumble in the heat; almond-paper
clouds gather low in the sky.

And it is the wind – squirrelling in
like something in the mind,
and carrying with it this larchy

kind of smell – that makes the mood
that makes the day
feel possible or probable

or credible or credulous. Below the trees
the shadow puddles out.
Numbly the light passes. Numbly

the wind slackens off into the morning.
The sound of insects
carries patiently into the air.

Section 6: Extension of thought

The girl beneath the orange-tree
makes out the smell
of attics and landings

and kitchens and pantries
that follows through
the sedges where the nettles

in the sun waver a little
and the shadows unscroll.
The clean, late-morning light

reflected above the brackens and
brambles feels freshest
where the powder-plants

bundle out over the lawns,
jellying like sugar
in the clearer, denser air.

Raucously delta-bugs
rumble in the heat; powder-paper
clouds gather low in the sky.

And it is the wind – fussing about
like something in the mind,
and carrying with it this willowy

kind of smell – that makes the mood
that makes the day
feel unpredicted, unexpected,

unguessed, unforeseen. Below the trees
the shadow puddles out.
Patiently the light passes. Patiently

the wind slackens off into the morning.
The sound of insects
carries awkwardly into the air.

Section 7: Creative thought

The girl beneath the orange-tree
makes out the smell
of metal or paper

or water or suede
that follows through
the fences where the nettles

in the sun flurry a little
and the shadows refract.
The clean, late-morning light

reflected above the brackens and
brambles feels gentlest
where the dabble-plants

bundle out over the lawns,
jellying like sugar
in the clearer, firmer air.

Raucously soda-bugs
rumble in the heat; linen-paper
clouds gather low in the sky.

And it is the wind – washing around
like something in the mind,
and carrying with it this coniferous

kind of smell – that makes the mood
that makes the day
feel theoretical and academic,

notional or presumed. Below the trees
the shadow puddles out.
Awkwardly the light passes. Awkwardly

the wind slackens off into the morning.
The sound of insects
carries freely into the air.

Division two: Communication of ideas

Section 1: Nature of ideas communicated

The girl beneath the orange-tree
makes out the smell
of rayon or nylon,

acrylic or cotton
that follows through
the flowers where the nettles

in the sun quiver a little
and the shadows shorten.
The clean, late-morning light

reflected above the brackens and
brambles feels richest
where the scatter-plants

bundle out over the lawns,
jellying like sugar
in the clearer, fuller air.

Raucously bug-bugs
rumble in the heat; framing-paper
clouds gather low in the sky.

And it is the wind – following in
like something in the mind,
and carrying with it this rowan-nut

kind of smell – that makes the mood
that makes the day
feel allusive or substantial

coherent or clear. Below the trees
the shadow puddles out.
Freely the light passes. Freely

the wind slackens out into the morning.
The sound of insects
carries reticently into the air.

Section 2: Modes of communication

The girl beneath the orange-tree
makes out a smell
like cabbages or kerosene

or pepper or eggs
that follows through
the grasses where the nettles

in the sun weaken a little
and the shadows resettle.
The clean, late-morning light

reflected above the brackens and
brambles feels hardest
where the rattle-plants

bundle out over the lawns,
jellying like sugar
in the clearer, warmer air.

Raucously hippo-bugs
rumble in the heat; tracing-paper
clouds gather low in the sky.

And it is the wind – colouring in
like something in the mind,
and carrying with it this rowanberry

kind of smell – that makes the mood
that makes the day
feel explicit and conspicuous

and definite and stark. Below the trees
the shadow puddles out.
Reticently the light passes. Reticently

the wind slackens out into the morning.
The sound of insects
carries deniably into the air.

The girl beneath the orange-tree
makes out a smell
like vitamins or poppies

or salt or limes
that follows through
the orchards where the nettles

in the sun dampen a little
and the shadows reduce.
The clean, late-morning light

reflected above the brackens and
brambles feels mildest
where the minnow-plants

bundle out over the lawns,
jellying like sugar
in the clearer, drier air.

Raucously sofa-bugs
rumble in the heat; baker-paper
clouds gather low in the sky.

And it is the wind – circling in
like something in the mind,
and carrying with it this rowan-bush

kind of smell – that makes the mood
that makes the day
feel grammatical and accurate,

transparent and precise. Below the trees
the shadow puddles out.
Deniably the light passes. Deniably

the wind slackens out into the morning.
The sound of insects
carries lushly into the air.

Class five: Volition: The exercise of the will

Division one: Individual volition

Section 1: Volition in general

The dogs beyond the orange-trees
take up the smell
of morphine or amphetamine

or iodine or codeine
that follows through
the rushes where the bean-vines

in the sun gesture a little
and the shadows combine.
The worn, late-morning light

arriving above the brackens and
brambles seems shrewdest
where the flannel-plants

bundle out over the lawns,
honeying like sugar
in the wider, bluer air.

Desperately drummer-bugs
stumble in the heat; carbon-paper
clouds gather low in the sky.

And it is the wind – rushing on
like something in the mind,
and carrying with it this ailanthus

kind of smell – that makes the mood
that makes the day
feel unasked and unbidden,

unprompted and unwilled. Below the trees
the shadow puddles out.
Lushly the light passes. Lushly

the wind slackens off into the morning.
The sound of insects
carries cleanly into the air.

Section 2: Prospective volition

The dogs beyond the orange-trees
take up the smell
of coffee-grounds and laundered shirts

and pilchards and milk
that follows through
the willows where the bean-vines

in the sun stifle a little
and the shadows unsettle.
The worn, late-morning light

arriving above the brackens and
brambles seems sharpest
where the rabble-plants

bundle out over the lawns,
honeying like sugar
in the wider, realer air.

Desperately gully-bugs
stumble in the heat; table-paper
clouds gather low in the sky.

And it is the wind – burrowing down
like something in the mind,
and carrying with it this oaky

kind of smell – that makes the mood
that makes the day
feel volitional or teleological,

deliberate or intent. Below the trees
the shadow puddles out.
Cleanly the light passes. Cleanly

the wind slackens off into the morning.
The sound of insects
carries cautiously into the air.

Section 3: Voluntary action

The dogs beyond the orange-trees
take up the smell
of detergents and aluminium,

elastoplast and wire wool
that follows through
the hedges where the bean-vines

in the sun soften a little
and the shadows retract.
The worn, late-morning light

arriving above the brackens and
brambles seems crudest
where the skittle-plants

bundle out over the lawns,
honeying like sugar
in the wider, wholer air.

Desperately blue-bugs
stumble in the heat; treacle-paper
clouds gather low in the sky.

And it is the wind – furrowing out
like something in the mind,
and carrying with it this green-apple

kind of smell – that makes the mood
that makes the day
feel restless and resolute,

vigorous and brisk. Below the trees
the shadow puddles out.
Cautiously the light passes. Cautiously

the wind slackens off into the morning.
The sound of insects
carries unnoticeably into the air.

Section 4: Antagonism

The dogs beyond the orange-trees
take up a smell
like pipe-smoke and pot-smoke

and wood-smoke and peat-smoke
which follows through
the mosses where the bean-vines

in the sun gladden a little
and the shadows remove.
The worn, late-morning light

arriving above the brackens and
brambles seems roughest
where the whistle-plants

bundle out over the lawns,
honeying like sugar
in the wider, nearer air.

Desperately lucky-bugs
stumble in the heat; ginger-paper
clouds gather low in the sky.

And it is the wind – bustling around
like something in the mind,
and carrying with it this crab-apple

kind of smell – that makes the mood
that makes the day
feel difficult and complex,

unyielding and obscure. Below the trees
the shadow puddles out.
Unnoticeably the light passes. Unnoticeably

the wind slackens off into the morning.
The sound of insects
carries naturally into the air.

Section 5: Results of action

The dogs beyond the orange-trees
take up the smell
of mayonnaise and nectarines

and solder and tar
that follows through
the sedges where the bean-vines

in the sun yellow a little
and the shadows expire.
The worn, late-morning light

arriving above the brackens and
brambles seems coldest
where the winnow-plants

bundle out over the lawns,
honeying like sugar
in the wider, denser air.

Desperately summer-bugs
stumble in the heat; rhubarb-paper
clouds gather low in the sky.

And it is the wind – hastening in
like something in the mind,
and carrying with it this dried-apple

kind of smell – that makes the mood
that makes the day
feel unfinished, unrealised,

undone, unbegun. Below the trees
the shadow puddles out.
Naturally the light passes. Naturally

the wind slackens off into the morning.
The sound of insects
carries certainly into the air.

Division two: Social volition

Section 1: General social volition

The dogs beyond the orange-trees
take up the smell
of coffee-rooms and reading-rooms,

recital-rooms and meeting-rooms
that follows through
the fences where the bean-vines

in the sun neaten a little
and the shadows contort.
The worn, late-morning light

arriving above the brackens and
brambles seems meanest
where the pingpong-plants

bundle out over the lawns,
honeying like sugar
in the wider, firmer air.

Desperately nonsense-bugs
stumble in the heat; raffia-paper
clouds gather low in the sky.

And it is the wind – rushing in
like something in the mind,
and carrying with it this appley

kind of smell – that makes the mood
that makes the day
feel loose or lax,

or feeble and weak. Below the trees
the shadow puddles out.
Certainly the light passes. Certainly

the wind slackens out into the morning.
The sound of insects
carries unhastily into the air.

Section 2: Special social volition

The dogs beyond the orange-trees
take up a smell
like fresh concrete setting

in the august weather
that follows through
the flowers where the bean-vines

in the sun giddy a little
and the shadows compose.
The worn, late-morning light

arriving above the brackens and
brambles seems suddenest
where the patter-plants

bundle out over the lawns,
honeying like sugar
in the wider, fuller air.

Desperately coco-bugs
stumble in the heat; feather-paper
clouds gather low in the sky.

And it is the wind – burrowing in
like something in the mind,
and carrying with it this sprucy

kind of smell – that makes the mood
that makes the day
feel legal or licensed,

complacent or indulgent. Below the trees
the shadow puddles out.
Unhastily the light passes. Unhastily

the wind slackens out into the morning.
The sound of insects
carries difficultly into the air.

The dogs beyond the orange-trees
take up a smell
like camphor or sulphur

or soda or soil
that follows through
the grasses where the bean-vines

in the sun ripen a little
and the shadows untangle.
The worn, late-morning light

arriving above the brackens and
brambles seems straightest
where the dangle-plants

bundle out over the lawns,
honeying like sugar
in the wider, warmer air.

Desperately snow-bugs
stumble in the heat; cellar-paper
clouds gather low in the sky.

And it is the wind – furrowing in
like something in the mind,
and carrying with it this mahogany

kind of smell – that makes the mood
that makes the day
feel observant and adherent,

religious and exact. Below the trees
the shadow puddles out.
Difficultly the light passes. Difficultly

the wind slackens out into the morning.
The sound of insects
carries gently into the air.

Section 4: Possessive relations

The dogs beyond the orange-trees
take up the smell
that drifts in from the river

when the weather's right,
and follows through
the orchards where the bean-vines

in the sun blunder a little
and the shadows renew.
The worn, late-morning light

arriving above the brackens and
brambles seems greatest
where the wafer-plants

bundle out over the lawns,
honeying like sugar
in the wider, drier air.

Desperately yellow-bugs
stumble in the heat; window-paper
clouds gather low in the sky.

And it is the wind – bustling in
like something in the mind,
and carrying with it this deciduous

kind of smell – that makes the mood
that makes the day
feel common or immovable,

fertile or fruitful. Below the trees
the shadow puddles out.
Gently the light passes. Gently

the wind slackens out into the morning.
The sound of insects
carries generously into the air.

Class six: Emotion, religion and morality

Section 1: General

The gardens round the orange-tree
bring out a smell
like honey and pumpkins

and rainstorms and soap
which carries through
the willows where the rushes

in the sun freshen a little
and the shadows meander.
The weak, late-morning light

assembling above the brackens and
brambles is warmest
where the haggle-plants

bundle out over the lawns,
rippling like sugar
in the bluer, realer air.

Breezily russet-bugs
bumble in the heat; breakfast-paper
clouds gather low in the sky.

And it is the wind – chasing away
like something in the mind,
and carrying with it this redwoody

kind of smell – that makes the mood
that makes the day
feel formed or framed

or moulded or shaped. Below the trees
the shadow puddles out.
Generously the light passes. Generously

the wind loosens off into the day.
The sound of insects
carries clearly into the air.

Section 2: Personal emotion

The gardens round the orange-tree
bring out a smell
like ethanol or barbitol

or luminol or lysol
that carries through
the hedges where the rushes

in the sun strengthen a little
and the shadows open.
The weak, late-morning light

assembling above the brackens and
brambles is softest
where the brandy-plants

bundle out over the lawns,
rippling like sugar
in the bluer, wholer air.

Breezily samba-bugs
bumble in the heat; brandy-paper
clouds gather low in the sky.

And it is the wind – cancelling out
like something in the mind,
and carrying with it this boxwoody

kind of smell – that makes the mood
that makes the day
feel peppy or perky

or pulpy or sharp. Below the trees
the shadow puddles out.
Clearly the light passes. Clearly

the wind loosens off into the day.
The sound of insects
carries rhythmically into the air.

The gardens round the orange-tree
bring out the smell
of nicotine and pencils

and adhesives and paint
that carries through
the mosses where the rushes

in the sun wriggle a little
and the shadows narrow.
The weak, late-morning light

assembling above the brackens and
brambles is purest
where the dawdle-plants

bundle out over the lawns,
rippling like sugar
in the bluer, nearer air.

Breezily holy-bugs
bumble in the heat; cable-paper
clouds gather low in the sky.

And it is the wind – bristling in
like something in the mind,
and carrying with it this yellow-wood

kind of smell – that makes the mood
that makes the day
feel easy and cosy

and clubby and couth. Below the trees
the shadow puddles out.
Rhythmically the light passes. Rhythmically

the wind loosens off into the day.
The sound of insects
carries carefully into the air.

Section 4: Morality

The gardens round the orange-tree
bring out the smell
of chlorides and fluorides

and bromides and oxides
that carries through
the sedges where the rushes

in the sun murmur a little
and the shadows ruffle.
The weak, late-morning light

assembling above the brackens and
brambles is dimmest
where the monkey-plants

bundle out over the lawns,
rippling like sugar
in the bluer, denser air.

Breezily window-bugs
bumble in the heat; washing-paper
clouds gather low in the sky.

And it is the wind – banking down
like something in the mind,
and carrying with it this greenwood

kind of smell – that makes the mood
that makes the day
feel detached and dispassionate,

neutral and moral. Below the trees
the shadow puddles out.
Carefully the light passes. Carefully

the wind loosens off into the day.
The sound of insects
carries meticulously into the air.

The gardens round the orange-tree
bring out a smell
like glue or electrics

or paracetamol or linen
that carries through
the fences where the rushes

in the sun stifle a little
and the shadows spoil.
The weak, late-morning light

assembling above the brackens and
brambles is simplest
where the rooster-plants

bundle out over the lawns,
rippling like sugar
in the bluer, firmer air.

Breezily ruckus-bugs
bumble in the heat; oyster-paper
clouds gather low in the sky.

And it is the wind – flowing out
like something in the mind,
and carrying with it this hill-wood

kind of smell – that makes the mood
that makes the day
feel perpetual and immeasurable,

spiritual and divine. Below the trees
the shadow puddles out.
Meticulously the light passes. Meticulously

the wind loosens off into the day.
The sound of insects
carries unhurriedly into the air.